Little Business Books

Teamwork

Written by **Ruth Percival**

Illustrated by **Dean Gray**

Published in 2026 by Windmill Books,
an Imprint of Rosen Publishing
2544 Clinton St.
Buffalo, NY 14224

First published in Great Britain in 2024 by Hodder & Stoughton
Copyright © Hodder & Stoughton Limited, 2024

Credits
Series Editor: Amy Pimperton
Series Designer: Peter Scoulding
Consultant: Philippa Anderson
Philippa Anderson has a business degree and is a writer and communications consultant who advises multinationals. She authors and contributes to business books.

Cataloging-in-Publication Data
Names: Percival, Ruth, author. | Grey, Dean, illustrator.
Title: Teamwork / Ruth Percival, illustrated by Dean Grey.
Description: Buffalo, NY : Windmill Books, 2026. | Series: Little business books | Includes glossary and index.
Identifiers: ISBN 9781725396586 (pbk.) | ISBN 9781725396593 (library bound) | ISBN 9781725396609 (ebook)
Subjects: LCSH: Cooperation--Juvenile literature. | Teams in the workplace--Juvenile literature. | Life skills--Juvenile literature. | Success--Juvenile literature. | Leadership--Juvenile literature.
Classification: LCC HD2963.P478 2026 | DDC 302'.14--dc23
All rights reserved.

All facts and statistics were up to date at the time of press.

No part of this book may be reproduced in any form without permission in writing from the publisher, except by a reviewer.

Printed in the United States of America

CPSIA Compliance Information: Batch #CSWM26
For Further Information contact Rosen Publishing at 1-800-237-9932

Contents

4	What Is Teamwork?
6	Be a Good Leader
8	Feel Motivated
10	Ask for Help
12	Listen to Others
14	Talk to Each Other
16	Share Your Ideas
18	Trust Your Team
20	Know What to Do
22	Welcome New People
24	Team Up
26	Succeed Together
28	Reward Success
30	Teamwork and You
31	Notes for Sharing This Book
32	Glossary

What Is Teamwork?

Teamwork means working together.

You need others to play games, such as hide-and-seek. A choir sounds great when they sing together. A football team works together to score goals and win a match.

Good teamwork needs skills, such as listening to others and doing things in a fair way.

Why does teamwork matter?

In business, teamwork is very important. It might mean trusting others to do a good job or solving a problem together.

For you, teamwork might be working as a class on a big project or being part of a sports team.

What will our animal friends find out about teamwork in business and about themselves?

Be a Good Leader

Things are about to go wrong at Monkey Adventures!

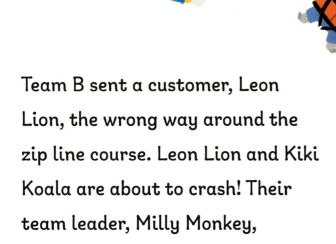

Team B sent a customer, Leon Lion, the wrong way around the zip line course. Leon Lion and Kiki Koala are about to crash! Their team leader, Milly Monkey, stays calm.

Everybody, stop!

Milly Monkey helps her teams to work together to fix the problem.

A good team leader stays calm when things go wrong.

Feel Motivated

Today, Pip Penguin's team is not working hard.
They don't feel motivated to find new customers.

But Pip has a way to encourage them ...

If you find ten new customers today, you can leave work early!

Ask for Help

Enzo Elephant is very busy. Owning a toy shop means he has to do EVERYTHING by himself ... or does it?

Enzo Elephant asks Wei Wolf to help.

As well as serving customers, can you open and close the shop every day, too?

Wei is happy to have more responsibility.

Enzo is glad he asked for help.
As a team, Enzo and Wei now share the work fairly.

Ask your teammates for help when you need it.

Listen to Others

Chip Cheetah's yoga instructor team is unhappy. Milly Monkey decides to complain.

But Chip isn't listening.

When Omar Owl and Kit Kangaroo complain, too, Chip finally listens.

Chip learned a lesson. Now he knows that listening shows he cares about what his team has to say.

Listening is an important teamwork skill.

Talk to Each Other

Oh no! The restaurant orders and takeout orders at Peter Panda's Pizza are all mixed up.

Peter Panda's team members talk to each other to work out a plan. Together, they decide to put the takeout orders and the restaurant orders on separate piles.

Talking helps a team to be organized.

Share Your Ideas

Tilly Tiger's shoe design team is very creative. But Tilly thinks that sharing their ideas could be great for her business.

Milly Monkey's shoe design is cool. Chip Cheetah's shoes are red. And Pip Penguin's shoes have flashing lights!

Tilly Tiger's team members inspired each other. Sharing ideas is fun!

When you share ideas, the whole team benefits.

Trust Your Team

Wei Wolf is annoying his Top Hats team.

He keeps checking up on them.

Know What to Do

Pip Penguin and Kiki Koala are confused. They both think it's their job to serve the drinks in Kit Kangaroo's café.

Kit Kangaroo's team needs to know which job each animal does, so that they don't get mixed up.

With Pip Penguin and Kiki Koala working well together, the café is running perfectly!

Knowing what you need to do is great for the whole team.

Welcome New People

Omar Owl decides to hire Leon Lion to help him run his kite-making business.

Leon is an expert kite-maker in his home country of Kenya.

Omar Owl's team is impressed. They haven't seen a kite like this before. Leon Lion's kite inspires them to try new designs of their own.

Welcoming new people to your team helps everyone to try new ideas.

Team Up

A very important customer has ordered a snow statue. It will be the biggest statue Peggy Polar Bear's team has ever built!

The Big Statue Team starts work, but there's a problem. The statue has lots of small details and pieces.

We need the Small Statue Team's help.

The two teams work together – and build an amazing statue!

When you team up, you can solve problems together.

Succeed Together

Kiki Koala's tree farm business is expensive to run.

One day, Kiki sees bees buzzing around the trees.

This gives her an idea.

Enzo pays Kiki rent money to put his beehives on her farm and open a honey shop.

Enzo and Kiki's partnership gets more customers. Their partnership means both businesses succeed.

A partnership is a way for two teams to succeed.

Reward Success

Leon Lion's Roarsome Cars sold lots of cars this year. Leon gave himself a sports car to celebrate his success.

Leon thinks his team members must be very pleased about his success. But they are not!

Oops! Leon Lion forgot that success depends on the whole team. He gives them a sports car, too.

It feels good to celebrate success with your whole team!

Teamwork and You

Our animal friends have learned a lot about teamwork in business. What they have learned can help you, too!

Chip Cheetah listened. Listening shows that you care about others. Listening can help to solve problems, too!

Tilly Tiger's team shared their ideas. Sharing ideas is fun and inspiring.

Omar Owl welcomed someone new. Being new to a team can feel scary. If a new person joins your team or class, always try to make them feel welcome.

Notes for Sharing This Book

This book introduces business ideas around the topic of teamwork, which link to core personal and social teamwork skills, such as listening, trust, and collaborating.

Talk to the child or class about what business is and why we need good businesses. You can use each scenario to discuss teamwork themes. For example, talk about how the child feels when taking part in group activities.

Teamwork succeeds when we are open to new ideas and experiences. Teamwork also relies on trusting others and speaking up. Talk about a time when the child worked on a class or group project. Did they enjoy being part of a team, or learn any new skills, such as being a team leader?

Glossary

benefit an advantage or an improvement in something

business a company that buys, makes, or sells goods or services to make money

choir a group of people who sing together

customer someone who buys things from a business

expert someone who is very skilled at something; someone who knows a lot about a topic

hire to take on someone to work for you

inspired to feel like you want to do something

motivated to feel enthusiastic about doing something

partnership when two or more businesses work together to help both succeed

rent a payment made so that you can use something that belongs to someone else - such as a house or land

responsibility the things you have to do as part of your job

succeed to reach a goal